EVERYTHING
YOU
KNOW
ABOUT
DINOSAURS
IS
WRONG!

DR NICK CRUMPTON
and GAVIN SCOTT

nosy
crow

FOR S. P. (FOR EVERYTHING)

N. C.

**FOR EVERYONE AT
ST JOHN'S FIRST SCHOOL IN FROME**

G. S.

First published 2021 by Nosy Crow Ltd
The Crow's Nest, 14 Baden Place, Crosby Row
London, SE1 1YW
www.nosycrow.com

ISBN 978 1 78800 810 5

Text © Nick Crumpton 2021
Illustrations © Gavin Scott 2021

With thanks to Susie Maidment at the Natural History Museum, Elsa Panciroli, Mike Taylor, Phil Mannion,
Thomas Halliday, James Neenan and all the dinosaur palaeontologists included
who prove dinosaurs aren't just for boys.

Very special thanks to my colleague and friend Jon Tennant – N. C.

Printed in China.
Papers used by Nosy Crow are made from wood
grown in sustainable forests.

1 3 5 7 9 8 6 4 2

CONTENTS

INTRODUCTION

The dinosaurs were animals that ruled the Earth for millions of years, during a time called the Mesozoic era, until they were all wiped out in a mass extinction 66 million years ago. Everyone knows that!

Now why on earth are you holding ANOTHER book about dinosaurs? Don't you know everything about *TYRANNOSAURUS*, *TRICERATOPS* and *DIPLODOCUS* already?

Well, this book is here to show you that, actually . . . everything you know about dinosaurs is *WRONG*!

Don't worry though – it's not your fault. It's because most of the facts you have learnt about dinosaurs have been told to you by grown-ups. But the thing about grown-ups is that they are all old . . . and the facts they know are old too!

And the funny thing about facts – especially old ones – is that, sometimes, they can be proved wrong when new discoveries are made.

In fact, the whole way science works is based on the idea that things can always be proved wrong if there's enough new evidence to show that they're not true. WHY is all this important?

Because over the last few years, scientists who study animals from the past, called palaeontologists, have discovered so many amazing, awesome, tiny, huge, weird, scary and cute new fossils of dinosaurs – now we KNOW that lots of things we THOUGHT we KNEW about dinosaurs are WRONG! So, fancy showing everyone how wrong they are? Get ready to UN-learn about dinosaurs!

ALL THE DINOSAURS LIVED AT THE SAME TIME

WRONG!

A lot of people think that all the dinosaurs lived at the same time: that dinosaurs like *STEGOSAURUS*, *TYRANNOSAURUS* and *PLATEOSAURUS* roamed the Earth together throughout the ages. In fact, different types of dinosaurs only lasted for two or three million years each, and only a few of the more famous dinosaurs ever lived together.

The dinosaurs lived during the *TRIASSIC*, *JURASSIC* and *CRETACEOUS* periods — huge blocks of time that stretched over the dizzyingly long *'MESOZOIC ERA'*. It's sometimes very hard to get your head around just how long this era — and the dinosaurs themselves — lasted.

PALAEOZOIC ERA
The geological era before the Mesozoic, lasting from 541 to 252 million years ago.

MASS EXTINCTION

MESOZOIC ERA
The time between about 252 to 66 million years ago, also known as 'The Age of Dinosaurs'.

TRIASSIC PERIOD
252–200 MILLION YEARS AGO

One of the very earliest dinosaurs we know about was *NYASASAURUS* from 243 million years ago. It was small and speedy, but we only know about it from a few bones. In fact, some palaeontologists aren't even sure if it was a true dinosaur, as it lived over 10 million years before other animals we know definitely were dinosaurs, like *EODROMAEUS* and *GNATHOVORAX*. The earliest dinosaurs we're sure were actually dinosaurs lived in the Late Triassic and it was during this time that we can find the ancestors of other, more famous dinosaurs.

JURASSIC PERIOD
200–145 MILLION YEARS AGO

During the Jurassic, the Earth was a wetter world than during the Triassic, and it was the period when the dinosaurs became very successful. It lasted a very long time – the distance in time between *DILOPHOSAURUS* and *BRACHIOSAURUS* was 40 million years!

In fact, dinosaurs like *TYRANNOSAURUS*, which appeared in the Cretaceous period, lived so long after the Jurassic dinosaurs like *STEGOSAURUS* that *TYRANNOSAURUS* lived closer in time to YOU than it did to them!

Dinosaurs from the beginning of the Mesozoic era and those at the end were separated by all this time, but palaeontologists, looking at lots of fossils together, love to track how dinosaurs evolved through time: how dinosaurs and their descendants changed shape. For example, *STEGOSAURUS* and its relative *ADRATIKLIT* looked quite similar, but parts of their skeleton as well as their spikes and plates, looked very different. They lived about 12 million years apart! To realise how long that is, 12 million years before today, giant ground sloths, three-toed horses and sabre-toothed tigers still walked the Earth!

Different dinosaurs lived at different times, and the length of time from the first to the last dinosaurs is almost impossible to understand. Palaeontologists only ever find fossils from tiny portions of time. Understanding the Mesozoic era is like trying to understand a whole story from just a few torn out pages of a book. The more fossils palaeontologists find, the more pages of the story they discover!

MASS EXTINCTION

CENOZOIC ERA
The current and most recent geological era, spanning 66 million years ago to the present day.

CRETACEOUS PERIOD
145–66 MILLION YEARS AGO

The Cretaceous was the time when the Earth began to look more like one we would recognise. More flowers evolved and the continents looked similar to how we see them today. By the start of this period, the dinosaurs had been on Earth for 100 million years – over 100 times longer than modern humans have existed for!

66 MILLION YEARS TO PRESENT DAY

ALL DINOSAURS BECAME FOSSILS

Everything we know about dinosaurs comes from fossils, so we depend a lot on finding them. But there's a problem . . . a bone becoming a fossil hardly EVER happens. It is an incredibly rare event and the chances of one single bone being fossilised is about one in a billion!

It's almost impossible for a bone to be fossilised if an animal lived in a dry place like up a mountain, or in a damp, moist place like a rainforest, where animals rot very quickly.

But at any one time during the Mesozoic era, perhaps millions of dinosaurs might have been alive all over the world.

And dinosaurs existed for millions of years! We've only been hunting for their fossils for just over 150 years so there must be hundreds of thousands of fossils still in the earth just waiting to be discovered!

AND every year the wind strips away more soil from the surface of the Earth, and the sea bashes away more rocks from the world's cliffs, which means we've still only seen the very top layer of fossils held within the ground.

Most fossils are found in very fine stones
which were once layers of squishy, soft mud.

The best fossil sites in the world were once floodplains
– areas of soggy land next to lakes or rivers. Like Auca
Mahuevo in Argentina (where *SALTASAURUS* was
discovered), or the Dinosaur National Monument in
North America (where *STEGOSAURUS* was excavated).

A lot of these places are now very dry. The rock gets worn
away quite quickly by the wind, exposing the glorious
fossils they have been hidden for millions of years.

Because dinosaurs were more likely to be fossilised near
to rivers, those that liked to drink and relax around these
areas – and the clumsy ones who would fall into the water
– are the ones we know about today.

All this means that pretty much every dinosaur that EVER lived disappeared
without a trace! Who knows what fascinating dinosaurs might have lived in
dry woodlands, arid deserts, and rocky mountains?

DINOSAURS ARE ONLY DUG UP IN DESERTS WRONG!

It's true that dinosaurs are often found on the surface of the Earth where plants don't cover the ground and soil has been removed – in places just like rocky deserts. Here, palaeontologists can get straight down to the ground to examine very old rock that sticks up above younger rock. But there are other places to find dinosaurs . . .

The exposed wall of a cliff is an excellent place to look back in time by looking closely at the ground. As waves crashed into the cliffs at Lavernock Point near Cardiff in Wales, they started slowly breaking down the stone to reveal the fossilised bones of the Triassic *DRACORAPTOR*!

But you don't need a crashing ocean to wear away the ground. The remains of the small ceratopsian *LEPTOCERATOPS* were discovered after floods wore away the banks of Red Deer River in Alberta, Canada.

It's very, very dangerous to search for fossils near cliffs – so please leave this to the professionals!

Digging into the ground is a sure-fire way to discover fossils. When miners were digging into the rocks of Canada looking for a type of oil, they discovered instead the fossilised remains of *BOREALOPELTA* complete with its skin, armour, snout and even fossilised lips!

Other mines are dug to search for different materials. *FULGUROTHERIUM* and *MUTTABURRASAURUS* from modern-day Australia were discovered by miners trying to find opal – a rare, blue stone some people like to wear as jewellery. Some of the dinosaurs' bones actually fossilised into this precious stone, which means they are very pretty . . .

Some places where palaeontologists find fossils are very hard to get to and haven't been visited by many people before.

On the slippy side of Mount Kirkpatrick near the Beardmore Glacier in Antarctica, palaeontologists needed to use a powerful jackhammer to discover *CRYOLOPHOSAURUS* in the thick polar rock.

It is very hard to work in Antarctica because of the frozen ground and terrible cold. *ANTARCTOPELTA* took almost 10 years to take out of the ground on James Ross Island, off the Antarctic Peninsula. Its name means 'Antarctic shield' because of its heavy armour and where it was discovered.

Traces of dinosaurs have been found on the Isle of Skye in the Inner Hebrides, off the coast of Scotland. A large collection of footprints were discovered on the tilted, rocky shore and palaeontologists clamber over miles of slippery, seaweed-covered rocks to study them. The coastline can be very blustery and cold in the winter, and swarming with midges in the summer!

Some places are much easier to find fossils in though. In Liaoning Province, Northeast China, a lot of beautiful fossils are found on hillsides by farmers, who discover delicate dinosaurs on thin slabs of rock on their land.

**Opal mines, polar islands and slippery cliffs . . .
so it's not just deserts after all!**

DINOSAURS ARE EXTINCT

WRONG!

So, the world suffered a catastrophe 66 million years ago when a HUGE space rock slammed into the Earth where Mexico is today, spewing millions of tonnes of rock and ash into the air, blocking out the sun.

The world became a horrible place to live, and this 'mass extinction event' was the end of the road for most of the dinosaurs . . . but not ALL of them became extinct.

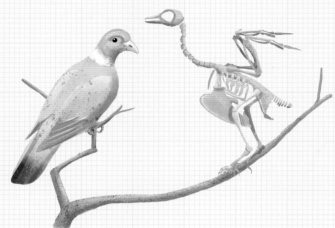

Yes . . . there are still dinosaurs alive today! And there might be one just outside your window. To help see how similar modern-day dinosaurs are to their ancient relatives let's think about a friendly neighbourhood pigeon. Because pigeons, like all birds, ARE dinosaurs.

Two-legged predators such as *BAMBIRAPTOR* already looked similar to modern birds under their skin, with fewer bones in their hands and a wishbone between their arms. But these dinosaurs had one thing modern birds don't have – teeth!

But, actually, lots of early birds had teeth. In fact, some early birds, like *ANCHIORNIS* and *XIAOTINGIA*, were so much like other non-flying dinosaurs they would have behaved and lived in very similar ways.

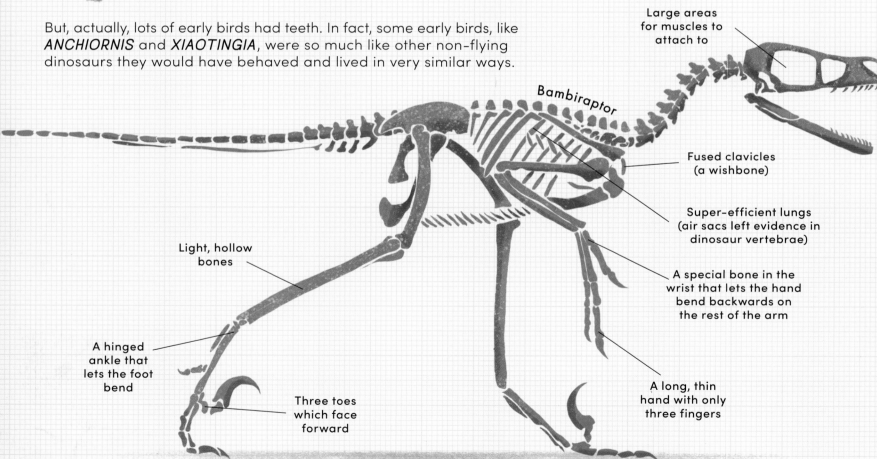

Large areas for muscles to attach to

Bambiraptor

Fused clavicles (a wishbone)

Super-efficient lungs (air sacs left evidence in dinosaur vertebrae)

Light, hollow bones

A special bone in the wrist that lets the hand bend backwards on the rest of the arm

A hinged ankle that lets the foot bend

Three toes which face forward

A long, thin hand with only three fingers

The Earth was a very tricky place to live after that asteroid slammed into it. Because birds' ancestors were much smaller than many other dinosaurs, they may have more easily been able to escape dangerous forest fires that erupted. Their beaks would have helped them eat difficult foods and their small size meant they could have babies more quickly than the larger dinosaurs. All this meant it was easier for them to survive in comparison to their bigger relatives.

Lots of birds had already evolved by the end of the Mesozoic era, but most didn't survive after the Cretaceous period and we only know about them thanks to their fossils.

The seed-eating *JEHOLORNIS* looked very different from modern birds as they still had long, bony tails!

Jeholornis

CONFUCIUSORNIS was the size of a dove and males attracted females by showing off their fancy tail streamers. They had very light bones, similar to birds today.

Confuciusornis

ALCMONAVIS was an early bird that had a skeleton and arm muscles that might have let it flap powerfully, something that other flying dinosaurs, like *ARCHAEOPTERYX*, couldn't have done well.

Alcmonavis

Some birds that lived in the Mesozoic have no ancestors today, like the long-snouted *SHANWEINIAO.*

Shanweiniao

Sapeornis

The large *SAPEORNIS* had teeth in their upper jaws, but not in the bottom. We also know it swallowed stones to help grind up its food!

From these beginnings, all the species of birds we know today, from hummingbirds to swans, from eagles to sparrows, slowly evolved. And each is an echo from an ancient age – dinosaurs are all around us!

13

DINOSAURS RULED THE EARTH

The 'Age of the Dinosaurs' started at the beginning of the Mesozoic era, during the Triassic period, right? Well, dinosaurs had some serious competition when they first evolved and weren't actually very important for most of the Triassic.

Dinosaurs (and birds) are a type of animal called an archosaur. There is another type of archosaur alive today – the crocodiles and alligators. These aren't very common in the wild now, apart from in places like Florida in the USA or sub-Saharan Africa, but back in the Triassic period, there would have been far more of the relatives of these reptiles around than dinosaurs.

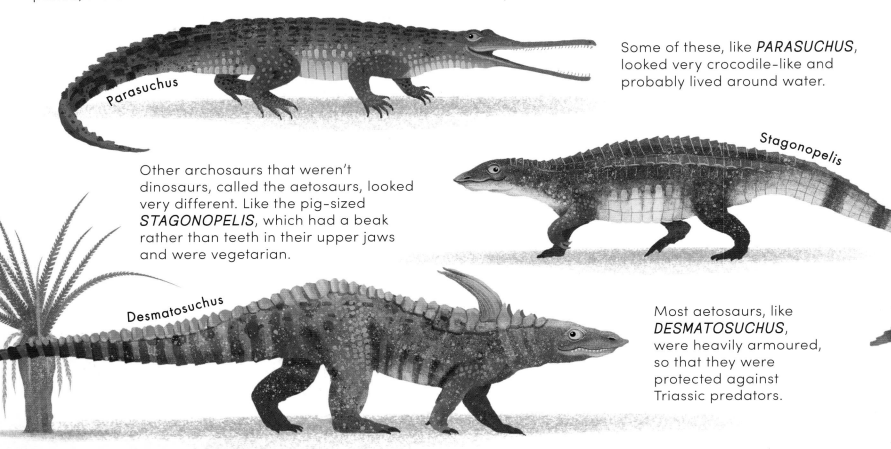

Parasuchus

Some of these, like *PARASUCHUS*, looked very crocodile-like and probably lived around water.

Stagonopelis

Other archosaurs that weren't dinosaurs, called the aetosaurs, looked very different. Like the pig-sized *STAGONOPELIS*, which had a beak rather than teeth in their upper jaws and were vegetarian.

Desmatosuchus

Most aetosaurs, like *DESMATOSUCHUS*, were heavily armoured, so that they were protected against Triassic predators.

Lotosaurus

The poposaurs were another group of non-dinosaur archosaurs that were common during the Triassic. Some, like *POPOSAURUS*, looked quite dinosaur-like . . .

Poposaurus

. . . whilst others, like *ARIZONASAURUS* and the herbivorous *LOTOSAURUS*, grew sails on their backs!

Rauisuchus

The most feared group of non-dinosaurs of the Triassic period would have been the rauisuchids. *RAUISUCHUS* was a huge, swift predator with an enormous, deep skull packed with teeth and muscle.

Postosuchus

POSTOSUCHUS probably moved around on its two back legs. It was over 4 metres long and would have hunted aetosaurs and maybe even early dinosaurs.

Saurosuchus

The closely related *SAUROSUCHUS* was even bigger and may have reached a huge length of 8 metres from tip to tail.

Because all of these other animals were already living on Earth, it was difficult for early dinosaurs to find their place. During the first half of the Triassic period, dinosaurs would have hidden in the shadows of the rauisuchids.

Dinosaurs finally got their lucky break after a terrible mass extinction about 220 million years ago and then another just over 201 million years ago, from which the crocodile-like archosaurs found it too difficult to recover.

With the fearsome poposaurs, the hungry aetosaurs and the terrifying rauisuchids out of the picture, dinosaurs were able to step into the footprints they left behind!

ALL DINOSAUR NAMES ARE HARD TO SAY

WRONG!

If you get your tongue tied in knots trying to say *PACHYCEPHALOSAURUS* (*pak-ee-SEF-uh-lo-SAWR-us*), *JIANIANHUALONG* (*j-YAN-yan-HWA-long*) or *NAASHOIBITOSAURUS* (*NA-a-SHOW-ee-BEET-o-SAWR-us*), don't worry! Not all dinosaur names are quite so tricky.

·ANZU·

ANZU was a large, toothless dinosaur from what is now North America. It was named after a half-lion, half-bird monster from an ancient Asian religion.

·MINMI·

MINMI was an armoured herbivore that lived in what is now Australia. It was named after the Minmi crossing, near where it was discovered.

·JOBARIA·

JOBARIA was a sauropod from Africa and was named after a mythical creature, Jobar, that people from Nigeria once believed in.

·WULONG·

WULONG was a small dinosaur related to *MICRORAPTOR*. 'Wu' means 'to dance' in Chinese, which describes the elegant, dance-like pose the fossilised skeleton was preserved in.

·SHANAG·

SHANAG was a small, speedy hunter and was named after a type of dance from a Buddhist festival.

·KHAAN·

KHAAN was discovered in Mongolia where 'khaan' is a word that means 'ruler' or 'king' (which makes it sound very impressive even though *KHAAN* wasn't actually very imposing!)

·YI·

YI has one of the shortest names scientists have ever given to an animal. Its full, scientific name is *YI QI*.

·THANOS·

THANOS was a huge carnivore named after a comic-book villain – poor *THANOS*!

·ZUUL·

ZUUL is another dinosaur named after a bad guy. It was an armoured dinosaur with a big tail club and was fossilised with skin! It was named after a character in the film *Ghostbusters* from the 1980s!

Often, the really long dinosaur names are made up of smaller words from languages like Mandarin, Greek and Latin. Once you've mastered these parts of dinosaur names you'll be able to recognise them and pronounce the longer names more easily. They also act as clues to tell you what sort of dinosaurs they were:

TYRANNUS . . .
(as in TYRANNOSAURUS – ty-RA-no-SAWR-us) means 'tyrant' (a sort of mean king or queen)

. . . LONG
(as in SHAOCHILONG – Sh-OW-chi-LONG) means 'dragon'

. . . SAURUS
(as in STEGOSAURUS – STEG-o-SAWR-us) means 'lizard' (even though dinosaurs aren't lizards!)

. . . RAPTOR
(as in APATORAPTOR –ah-PAT-o-RAP-tor) means 'thief' or 'robber'

. . . TITAN
(as in GIRAFFATITAN – gi-RAFF-o-TY-tan) means titanic or HUGE

. . . ORNIS
(as in SERIKORNIS – sery-CORN-is) means 'bird' – and is often used to mean 'like a bird'

. . . PHYSIS
(as in COELOPHYSIS – SEE-lo-FI-sis) means 'form'

. . . DON
(as in HYPSILOPHODON – HIP-si-LOF-o-DON) means 'tooth'

EO . . .
(as in EOTYRANNUS – E-O-ty-RANUS) means 'dawn' and is used for the earliest dinosaurs

. . . MIMUS
(as in ANSERIMIMUS – AN-sur-i-MY-mus) means 'mimic' or 'like'

. . . CERATOPS
(as in BAGACERATOPS – BAG-a-SERA-tops) means, literally, 'horn-face'!

. . . SUCHUS
(as in INDOSUCHUS – IN-do-SU-kas) means 'crocodile' and is often used to mean 'like a crocodile'

. . . ONYX
(as in DRACONYX – dra-CON-iks) means 'claw'

DINOSAURS WERE EITHER 'LIZARD-HIPPED' OR 'BIRD-HIPPED' WRONG?

Everyone who knows even a little bit about dinosaurs knows there are two main groups . . . and it's all in the hips.

Most dinosaur books tell you this: dinosaurs including sauropods like *KAATEDOCUS* and theropods like *BEISHANLONG* were saurischians, who had 'lizard-like' hip bones, whereas ornithopods like *OLOROTITAN* and ceratopsians like *AURORACERATOPS* were ornithischians, and had 'bird-like' hip bones.

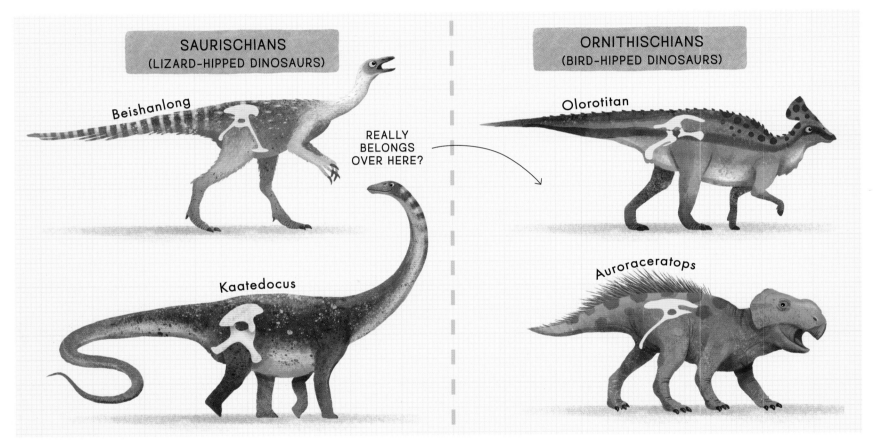

SAURISCHIANS
(LIZARD-HIPPED DINOSAURS)

Beishanlong

REALLY BELONGS OVER HERE?

Kaatedocus

ORNITHISCHIANS
(BIRD-HIPPED DINOSAURS)

Olorotitan

Auroraceratops

Well, to start, avian dinosaurs (or modern-day birds) evolved from animals that were saurischians . . . so 'bird-like hips' really should have been the name given to the 'lizard-hipped' saurischians!

But here's where it gets really interesting: some palaeontologists in 2017 scrapped 130 years of scientific knowledge and began to think that, maybe, this way of splitting the dinosaurs isn't quite right after all.

By painstakingly looking extremely closely at many dinosaur fossils, they began to think that the theropods might actually have been more closely related to the ornithischians than to the sauropods, and that theropods and ornithischians should be grouped together in a group of dinosaurs called the 'ornithoscelida' (which is a mouthful). Yeesh!

Not all palaeontologists agree with this idea though and only time will tell whether this new family tree is the correct one. In scientific language, this is a 'new hypothesis' to be tested and might be disproved by other scientists in the future . . .

Biologists (who study animals and plants alive today) and palaeontologists love to group animals together in little clubs. Some of these clubs are very large.

European mole

'Mammals', for instance, includes over 5,000 different sorts of animals. But these are made up of smaller groups, like 'talpids' – which is part of 'mammals' but only includes about 50 types of moles and their close relatives.

By grouping animals together by how similar they are to each other, scientists are able to make better sense of the animal kingdom – how different types of living things are related to each other and how they evolved over time.

The more biologists study animals, the more surprises can be found . . . For example, golden moles were long thought to be part of the 'talpid' gang, along with European moles and those that live in North America, but then scientists discovered that they actually belonged in a group of animals called 'afrotheria' – along with elephants! Which means golden moles are more closely related to elephants than they are to the dark-furred moles you might find making a mess in a garden north of the equator.

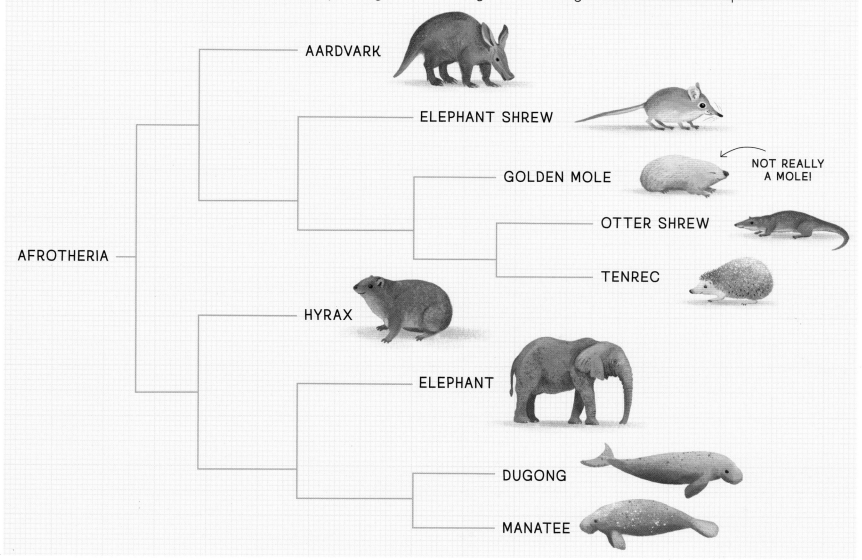

Sometimes it can be very difficult to find the parts of animals that unite them as these can be hidden deep inside them or in tiny details of their skeletons – like a hidden password – and this is doubly true for extinct animals, like dinosaurs.

So, even though we might THINK we know which animals are related to others in their family tree, sometimes this can be turned upside down . . . all in a shake of the hips!

ALL DINOSAURS WERE ENORMOUS

WRONG!

GIRAFFATITAN, TYRANNOSAURUS, DREADNOUGHTUS . . . although a lot of dinosaurs you can see in museums were gigantic, many of them were much, MUCH smaller.

Many small dinosaurs lived at the start of the Age of the Dinosaurs, but some dinky dinosaurs lived during the Cretaceous period, like the two-legged ornithopod *HAYA*.

But just how small is 'small'?

JINFENGOPTERYX was a fast, feathered theropod related to *STENONYCHOSAURUS* and may have been a herbivore (or at least we know it ate seeds from time to time).

Jinfengopteryx

Gasparinisaura

GASPARINISAURA was a small animal related to *IGUANODON* that was between 1 to 2 metres long, which was small in comparison to its relatives.

The stubby-armed alvarezsaurid dinosaurs were very small. *SHUVUUIA* and *PARVICURSOR* from Mongolia were tiny, speedy theropods. You'd need six *SHUVUUIA* just to balance one bag of sugar!

Parvicursor

Shuvuuia

DINO FACT!

1 cm

The smallest dinosaur footprints ever found are TINY – barely 1 centimetre long. They were found in Korea and were made by raptor-like dinosaurs.

Sometimes animals that are separated from the rest of their species evolve, or change, into smaller versions of their relatives, sometimes known as 'dwarf' species. This usually happens on islands, where there is less space to roam, fewer predators and less food to eat.

It looks like some dinosaurs were dwarf species too. By looking at fossilised bones and counting the number of 'growth rings' in them, palaeontologists can tell if dinosaurs were grown-ups or youngsters and it looks like these small dinosaurs were fully grown.

Diplodocus

Tethyshadros

TETHYSHADROS was a hadrosaur, a duck-billed dinosaur, discovered in modern-day Italy. It was only the size of a donkey (but with a longer tail).

Magyarosaurus

Europasaurus

MAGYAROSAURUS and *EUROPASAURUS* were dwarf sauropods. *EUROPASAURUS* probably lived on an island and so might not have needed to grow large to be protected from predators. *MAGYAROSAURUS* only grew to about 6 metres long which, for a sauropod, was tiny. After all, *DIPLODOCUS* was more like 26 metres long!

Although we now know that not all dinosaurs were giants, it makes sense that we know the most about all the big dinosaurs because the BIGGER a fossil is, the EASIER it is to find!

DINOSAURS WERE GREEN AND SCALY

 WRONG!

When dinosaurs were first described, early palaeontologists assumed they were most closely related to animals like lizards. This led them to believe that they were covered in lizard-like scales and were greeny brown. But as more has been discovered about dinosaur biology, it looks less likely that this is what dinosaur skin REALLY looked like . . .

Some dinosaurs were 'scaly', like the long-necked *HAESTASAURUS*. But their scales weren't like the overlapping scales found on many species of lizards but more like the bobbly, pebbly skin – like on the surface of a basketball – of Gila monsters from North America . . .

The skin of dinosaurs wouldn't have been rock-hard either, but similar to the soft, stretchy skin on a chickens' legs and feet.

Gila monster

Tianyuraptor

Palaeontologists now know that a lot of theropods, like *TIANYURAPTOR*, were covered with feathers – on their heads, arms and tails.

Dilong

Some dinosaurs, like *DILONG*, had very simple, fuzzy feathers called 'protofeathers', which might have kept them cosy and warm.

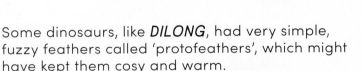

Gargoyleosaurus

Some other dinosaurs, like *GARGOYLEOSAURUS*, had large, horny scutes – like the bumps that cover a crocodile's skin – which were a lot more heavy-duty than scales!

Other dinosaurs, like *CAUDIPTERYX*, had more complicated feathers that looked like those of birds alive today, and even some huge predators, like *YUTYRANNUS*, were covered in plumage (but they still would have looked scary)!

Caudipteryx

Yutyrannus

In fact, lots of dinosaurs, not just theropods like these, had feathers. Although we don't think *TRICERATOPS* was fuzzy, we know that lots of its relatives, like *KULINDADROMEUS*, actually did have structures that looked a lot like simple feathers!

And were any dinosaurs actually green? By looking very, very closely at fossilised feathers, palaeontologists can tell what colour some dinosaurs really were!

ANCHIORNIS was a small dinosaur with white bars on its wings. It had a tall crest on top of its head which was a deep rusty-red colour.

The 'rainbow dinosaur' *CAIHONG* had very special kinds of feathers. They were iridescent, which means they looked like they were different colours depending on what angle you looked at them from.

SINOSAUROPTERYX had simple feathers that were a chestnut-brown colour. It had light stripes on its long tail and a dark pattern on its face, making it look like it wore a mask.

Modern-day birds can see a lot of colours, even some that humans can't see. They use these colours to send signs to other birds like 'stay away' and 'we should make a baby!'.

Dinosaurs could probably see colours in a similar way (including some ultraviolet colours that are invisible to humans), so animals like *GIGANTORAPTOR* may have used bright colours to 'talk' to each other too.

Some colours help animals blend into the background. This is called 'camouflage'. The fossilised skin of *PSITTACOSAURUS* showed microscopic clues to the animals' colour! It was mainly brown on top but paler underneath – like the fur of squirrels or deer today. This means it would have been really difficult to see and could stay hidden if it lived in a wood or forest.

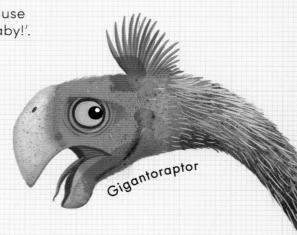

Gigantoraptor

So scientists don't ACTUALLY have any proof that dinosaurs were green and scaly. Instead, we now know that some dinosaurs were actually far more colourful – and feathery – than scientists had first thought!

DINOSAURS WEREN'T VERY SMART

WRONG!

One of the easiest ways to tell how intelligent animals are is to look at how big their brain is in comparison to the size of their body.

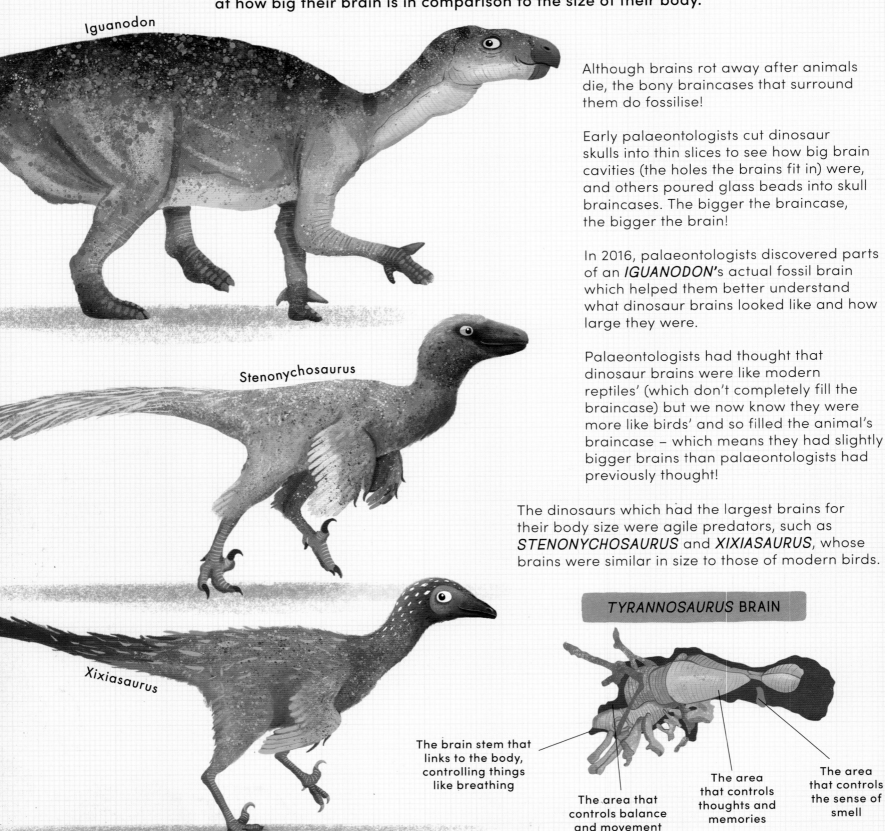

Iguanodon

Stenonychosaurus

Xixiasaurus

Although brains rot away after animals die, the bony braincases that surround them do fossilise!

Early palaeontologists cut dinosaur skulls into thin slices to see how big brain cavities (the holes the brains fit in) were, and others poured glass beads into skull braincases. The bigger the braincase, the bigger the brain!

In 2016, palaeontologists discovered parts of an *IGUANODON*'s actual fossil brain which helped them better understand what dinosaur brains looked like and how large they were.

Palaeontologists had thought that dinosaur brains were like modern reptiles' (which don't completely fill the braincase) but we now know they were more like birds' and so filled the animal's braincase – which means they had slightly bigger brains than palaeontologists had previously thought!

The dinosaurs which had the largest brains for their body size were agile predators, such as *STENONYCHOSAURUS* and *XIXIASAURUS*, whose brains were similar in size to those of modern birds.

TYRANNOSAURUS BRAIN

The brain stem that links to the body, controlling things like breathing

The area that controls balance and movement

The area that controls thoughts and memories

The area that controls the sense of smell

Although the size of an animal's whole brain is important, measuring the sizes of different parts of the brain can also help biologists understand how good dinosaurs were at different jobs.

Some dinosaurs that ate a mixed or plant-based diet, like the ostrich-like *HARPYMIMUS*, had very small olfactory bulbs. These are the parts of the brain which sense smells and it meant they could only eat food from plants which were easy to find.

Harpymimus

Buitreraptor

BUITRERAPTOR had much larger olfactory bulbs. These are bigger in animals with a brilliant sense of smell, like predators (which hunt other animals) that need to sniff out the animals they eat (their 'prey').

Zanabazar

Later theropods, like *ZANABAZAR*, had large brains and would have been great at problem-solving.

Although dinosaurs' brains weren't anything like as complex as mammals', having a bird-brain still meant dinosaurs would have been capable of some amazing behaviour. After all, modern-day birds can move together in flocks of thousands, migrate between countries without getting lost, mark their territories with intricate songs, and some can even make simple tools out of twigs . . .

DINOSAURS COULD ROAR

WRONG!

Did dinosaurs really make a deafening din? Looking at animals that roar today can give us clues to help us find out.

On the African savanna, a *LION*'s roar can be heard 8 kilometres away! The secret of the lion's roar is the special skin and vocal cords deep within its throat – and the roar can mean 'hello', 'where are you?' or 'stay back!'.

lion

Vegetarian animals can roar too, like male *RED DEER* that roar to show off about how big they are to other males – before clashing antlers!

red deer

RED HOWLER MONKEYS use a special bone in their throat to make their deep, loud roar, which can be heard almost 4 kilometres away, echoing above Central and South American jungles.

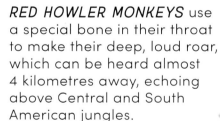

red howler monkey

harbour seal

It's not only land animals that can roar. *HARBOUR SEALS* are shy when they're on land, but under water they roar when they want to warn off intruders. Different groups of seals roar in their own way, like people speaking with different accents.

Those noisy animals were all mammals – but what about reptiles and birds that are alive today?

CROCODILES, ALLIGATORS and CAIMAN might look scary, but they can't really roar. The biggest noise they can make is a loud, deep rumble that makes water dance and splutter off their armoured backs.

crocodile

Komodo dragon

The dinosaurs alive today are known for their chirps, tweets and dawn choruses. The WHITE BELLBIRD from South America is the world's noisiest bird and makes a 'bonk' louder than amotorbike. But it's not a roar!

white bellbird

The world's biggest lizard is the KOMODO DRAGON from Indonesia. Although they hunt animals as big as water buffalo and pigs, they only make a menacing-sounding hiss from their toothy mouths.

Dinosaur voice boxes don't fossilise . . . If they did, we'd know for sure what sounds they made. But because these reptiles and birds are all related to dinosaurs, it means dinosaurs probably sounded similar.

Parasaurolophus

So, it is likely that TYRANNOSAURUS and ALLOSAURUS didn't actually roar . . . But some of the duck-billed hadrosaur dinosaurs, like PARASAUROLOPHUS, might have blown air around their strange head crests, which might have made them sound like . . . a trumpet! Toot-toot!

DINOSAURS WERE MEAN

WRONG!

We've all seen pictures of scary-looking *TYRANNOSAURUS* in books or models of grumpy-looking *STEGOSAURUS* in museums and it's hard to imagine them having a softer side. But there are a lot of fossil clues that tell us many dinosaurs had a caring side when it came to their babies.

Today, many species of living dinosaurs and their relatives, crocodiles and alligators, look after their young by fetching food for them and protecting them in cosy nests.

Mei

When they first hatch out of their eggs, baby birds, crocodiles and alligators aren't ready to fend for themselves so they need their parents to care for them.

It's likely many species of extinct dinosaurs, like *MEI*, looked and acted similarly when they hatched out of their eggs and needed their parents to help them survive.

By studying dinosaur footprints, palaeontologists know that herds of dinosaurs would travel with younger members of their species, and probably would have protected them from predators trying to pick off a tasty snack – just as large animals like elephants do today.

Maiasaura

MAIASAURA was a large duck-billed dinosaur that we know built mounds with lots of other mothers to keep their eggs and babies in. There are even fossils that suggest that they returned year after year to use the same spot as a nursery.

A lot of dinosaurs, like **TIANYURAPTOR** and **SERIKORNIS**, had feathers but could not fly. Perhaps many of them used their feathers like **CITIPATI**, to cover eggs and keep them at the right temperature.

Tianyuraptor

A fossil of **CITIPATI**, frozen in time, shows us how some dinosaurs sat on a lot of eggs, in a similar way to birds sitting on their eggs before they hatch. Although its spindly arms would not have protected them very well, the feathers that spanned over them would have.

Palaeontologists now think that this fossil of **CITIPATI** (which had been nicknamed 'Big Mama') was a male, and that he was actually babysitting many mothers' eggs, not just one.

Citipati

DINO FACT!

In 2020, palaeontologists made the amazing discovery that most dinosaur eggs were soft and only later dinosaurs evolved hard-shelled, bird-like eggs. Because soft shells wouldn't have fossilised very well, that could explain why palaeontologists haven't found very many dinosaur eggs.

Although many dinosaurs might have covered their eggs with earth and left the hatchlings to fend for themselves, these amazing fossils show that at least some dinosaur species stuck around to look after and bring up their kids. Not SO mean, after all!

LONG-NECKED DINOSAURS ALL LOOKED THE SAME

WRONG!

We ALL know what the sauropod dinosaurs looked like, right? They're the ones with long necks, long tails and big feet – just like *DIPLODOCUS*.

The earliest sauropods we have found – like *ISANOSAURUS* from the Triassic period and *KOTASAURUS* from the Jurassic period – already walked on four wide feet and had the long necks and swishing tails that make this group so easy to spot. But there were a lot of different kinds of sauropods – and some were really weird.

Brachytrachelopan

Being a chunky herbivore can be a scary business – all that standing around munching on vegetation can make you a prime target for predators. But some sauropods like *SHUNOSAURUS* had something they could use to defend themselves – a spike-covered club on the end of their tail. Take that, theropods!

BRACHYTRACHELOPAN had a very short neck and couldn't stretch it very far up or down.

Shunosaurus

SALTASAURUS went a little further – a lot of its body was covered in armour plates to protect it from attacks.

Bajadasaurus

Some other sauropods had crazy neck spikes – *BAJADASAURUS* was only about the height of an elephant but its neck spines would have made it look much bigger!

30

Although these dinosaurs definitely looked different from *DIPLODOCUS*, how do we even know what *DIPLODOCUS* really looked like?

DINO FACT!

These enormous sauropods all evolved from animals like the tiny *SATURNALIA* that lived in the Triassic period.

Saturnalia

Very new fossils have made some other palaeontologists believe that *DIPLODOCUS*'s eyes might have been protected from the sun by some bony eye-shades.

Recently found fossils have made some palaeontologists think that *DIPLODOCUS* had a horny beak which would have been helpful for stripping small leaves off trees.

DIPLODOCUS was only recently found to have had a row of 18-centimetre-long, hard, thin spikes running down its back.

Saltasaurus

Although most of *DIPLODOCUS*'s tail was held out straight, the end was very thin and would have hung limp like a whip. This might have been used as a pretty scary defence against predators.

The sauropods continued to evolve into strange forms until 66 million years ago, when they died out along with the rest of the non-bird dinosaurs. By the time they disappeared some species from what is now South America had become the largest animals ever to walk the Earth – life on land would NEVER be this big again!

TYRANNOSAURUS REX WAS THE BIGGEST PREDATOR

WRONG!

Let's be honest . . . *TYRANNOSAURUS* was pretty enormous.

The largest *TYRANNOSAURUS* skeletons ever to be discovered are nicknamed 'Scotty' and 'Sue' and are kept in museums in the USA and Canada.

Sue was huge – over 4 metres tall at the hips! Scotty was a bit stockier and, even though it died when only 30 years old, it could have weighed 8 tonnes. That's heavier than three white rhinos . . . or over 100 average-size grown-ups!

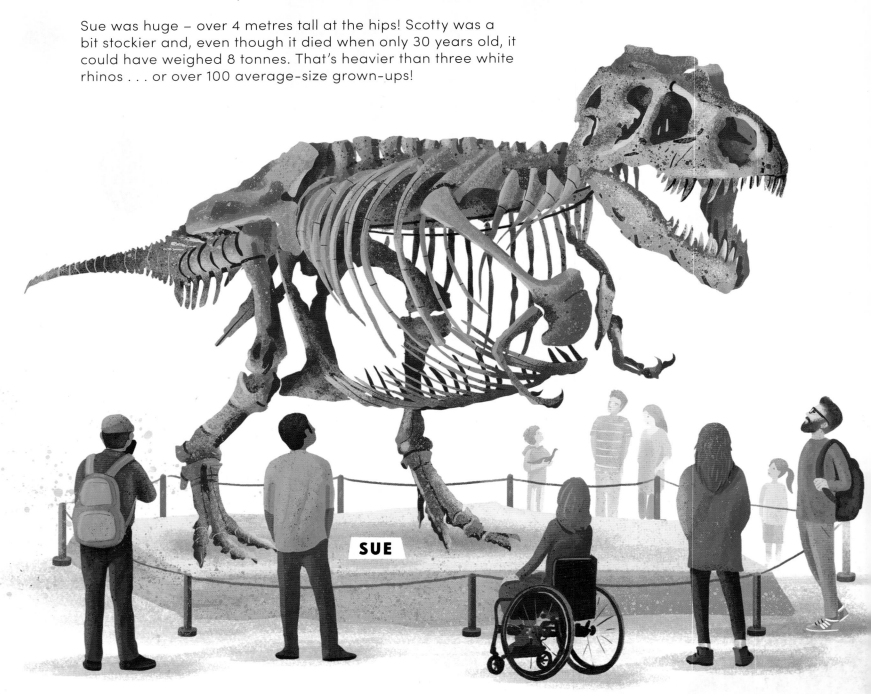

SUE

But was *TYRANNOSAURUS* really the largest of them all? Well, palaeontologists now think that there are some other dinosaurs that could be crowned 'Biggest Predator' instead. Dinosaurs like *CARCHARODONTOSAURUS* from Algeria and *GIGANOTOSAURUS* and *TYRANNOTITAN* from Argentina looked similar to *TYRANNOSAURUS*'s relative *ALLOSAURUS* but were much, much bigger!

It also depends how 'big' is measured. The gargantuan *SPINOSAURUS* holds the record for the longest theropod – it was over 15 metres from its snout to the tip of its tail. That's 3 metres longer than Sue!

SPINOSAURUS lived in and around water, like its relative *SIAMOSAURUS*, and ate fish with quick snaps of its jaws.

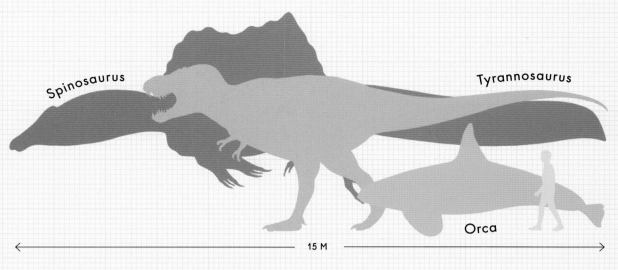

Spinosaurus

Tyrannosaurus

Orca

15 M

Working out exactly how massive dinosaurs were is a tricky business. Deciding how long dinosaurs were might seem easy, but hardly any dinosaur skeletons are found complete, so scientists have to make guesses about how many bones are missing and how they might fit together.

The weight of dinosaurs is even more complicated to work out! Some palaeontologists used to build little models of what they thought the dinosaurs might have looked like and put them in water to see how much water they displaced – like when you get in the bath and the water rises – to give them a clue to how heavy they were.

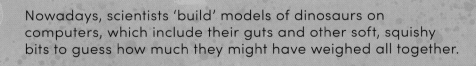

Nowadays, scientists 'build' models of dinosaurs on computers, which include their guts and other soft, squishy bits to guess how much they might have weighed all together.

What's important to remember is that dinosaurs, just like animals today, would have all been unique. One *CAMARASAURUS* might have been a bit bigger than usual, some a bit skinnier. One *TALARURUS* may have been a bit shorter, while some had longer legs . . .

Although *TYRANNOSAURUS* was pretty huge, it certainly had some competition for the title of 'Biggest Predator', and working out who was actually the biggest is a pretty tricky thing to do!

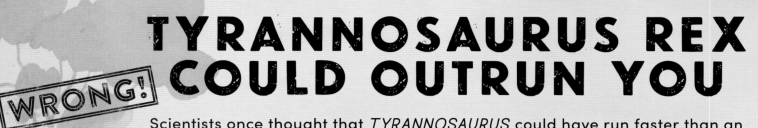

TYRANNOSAURUS REX COULD OUTRUN YOU

WRONG!

Scientists once thought that *TYRANNOSAURUS* could have run faster than an Olympic sprinter, which would have meant that this 6-tonne celebrity would have been an unstoppable hunting machine. But could it REALLY run that fast? How can we tell?

Dinosaur footprints have been found all over the world, from the Isle of Skye in the UK to Queensland, Australia, and they can tell us a lot about how dinosaurs moved.

By measuring the 'stride' distance between the footprints and having an idea of how big the dinosaur that made the tracks was, palaeontologists can guess how fast the animal was moving.

The further apart the footprints and narrower the track, the quicker the dinosaur! But it might have been difficult to run and walk on the sorts of sand and ground that make good fossils, so there aren't too many dinosaur trackways, or paths, to investigate.

Depending on how squishy the ground is, the shape of the footprints might change before becoming hard and this can sometimes confuse palaeontologists when they are trying to work out how big the dinosaurs were.

The best way to work out how fast an animal could run is by thinking about its muscles, but unfortunately dinosaur muscles don't fossilise.

Instead, palaeontologists look at animals alive today. Then they try to fill in what the muscles on dinosaurs might have looked like and imagine how powerfully they could pull back on the bones of the legs.

So, could *TYRANNOSAURUS* run quickly? Well, it had very long legs, which meant that it could stretch them quite far forwards and backwards, and, by working out where muscles would have attached to bones at the base of the tail and comparing this with muscles on modern birds and reptiles, palaeontologists now realise that *TYRANNOSAURUS* would have been able to walk for a long time.

But, being so big meant that running, or at least walking very quickly, could be downright dangerous – a *TYRANNOSAURUS* couldn't move very fast without the risk of shattering the bones in its feet and legs!

All of this adds up to show us that *TYRANNOSAURUS* could only move at . . . about 12 miles an hour – which YOU could probably run at, too! But running isn't everything. By studying their skeletons in museums, palaeontologists recently discovered that *TYRANNOSAURUS* was amazing at turning and pivoting very quickly, making it an extremely agile hunter!

With a head filled with razor-sharp teeth, jaws capable of smashing through bone, and the spinning skills of a ballerina, *TYRANNOSAURUS* may not have been the fastest dinosaur, but it was a MENACING predator and would have been well worth steering clear of.

DINOSAURS WERE COLD-BLOODED

WRONG!

'Cold-blooded' animals need the warmth of the sun to heat them up before they can start moving around. Nearly all modern-day snakes and lizards are cold-blooded, which is why you might have seen them 'basking' on a rock to warm up.

'Warm-blooded' animals, like mammals and birds, use instant-access heat energy from inside their bodies without having to worry about warming up first. For years, people had thought dinosaurs were all cold-blooded, but what do new fossils tell us?

Psittacosaurus

If dinosaurs were covered in feathers and fluff, as new fossils suggest, they would have been 'insulated', which means they would have easily kept the heat they had made inside their bodies. Warm-blooded animals today rely on their fur and feathers for exactly this reason.

Being warm-blooded lets animals stay busy for longer periods of time, but they need to be able to get blood to all parts of the body quickly to fuel this amount of activity. And that's exactly what the bones of dinosaurs show us they were able to do, by directing blood from their hearts around their bodies at very high pressure!

Warm-blooded animals grow much quicker than cold-blooded animals. By looking at bone growth rings (which are like the rings found inside a tree), palaeontologists have discovered that dinosaurs did in fact grow very quickly, and they used a lot of energy to do so!

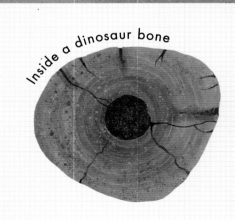

Inside a dinosaur bone

Because cold-blooded animals rely on the temperature around them to warm them up, it is very unusual to find them in chilly parts of the world. But we know that **NANUQSAURUS** lived and hunted where Alaska lies today, as well as the duck-billed hadrosaur **EDMONTOSAURUS**.

Nanuqsaurus

Although the Arctic wasn't as cold as it is now, it was still much chillier than other parts of the Earth in the Cretaceous period, so being warm-blooded would have been a big help!

At the other end of the world, **LEAELLYNASAURA** was a small polar dinosaur that lived within the Antarctic Circle. It would have needed to survive long periods of darkness in the southern winter without any opportunity to heat up in the sun, and so must have been warm-blooded to heat itself!

Finding these dinosaurs living in colder places, as well as evidence of feathers and fast growth, has made many palaeontologists think that some dinosaurs, if not all of them, were warm-blooded . . . and wouldn't have needed to lie out in the sun to catch those rays!

Leaellynasaura

DINOSAURS ONLY LIVED ON LAND

WRONG!

OK, clever claws. So there are lots of prehistoric animals that less-than-expert people sometimes mistake for dinosaurs, and you MIGHT already know that pterosaurs (the reptiles that flew in the sky on bat-like wings) and plesiosaurs (the long-necked hunters that swam in the oceans) weren't actually dinosaurs.

But brand-new fossils show that some dinosaurs were picky when it came to where they liked to live – and not all of them had their feet on the ground.

Although *HALSZKARAPTOR* had strong legs, which meant it could run well, it spent a lot of its time on the water, like ducks do today. Its spoon-shaped snout at the end of its swan-like neck was jam-packed full of sharp teeth to help it grab on to slippery prey.

If you're going to spend your time tromping through squishy mud along riverbanks, it helps to have long, spread-out toes to help you distribute your weight, just like wading birds like avocets and moorhens today – and that's just what the feet of *ANZU* looked like!

Halszkaraptor

Anzu

Some dinosaurs liked to live under the ground. *ORYCTODROMEUS* was a small, herbivorous animal that lived in snug burrows about 2 metres long, and looked after their babies in these cosy homes.

Oryctodromeus

Living in trees is a great way to avoid predators and find new types of tasty food. Today, lots of animals – from baby Komodo dragons to some types of goats – spend at least some of their time up in the branches!

With fleshy skin almost like wings draped between their long fingers, *YI* and *AMBOPTERYX* looked a little like bats do today. These dinosaurs could probably glide between the trees, hunting insects and small reptiles.

Having long fingers is a big help if you spend your time in trees. *SCANSORIOPTERYX* had huge hands and palaeontologists now think it used them for holding on to branches.

Scansoriopteryx

Ambopteryx

Dinosaurs like *EPIDEXIPTERYX* had long arms from the time they hatched. They also had long, curved claws to hold on to branches. They may have used their hard tails to help them balance, just like woodpeckers do today.

Microraptor

Epidexipteryx

MICRORAPTOR probably couldn't beat its wings, but having four wings rather than two meant it could glide from tree to tree as it hunted species of early birds!

DINO FACT!

In 2020, palaeontologists discovered a new *SPINOSAURUS* skeleton that showed that it had a long tail that looked like a crocodile's and could have been used to help it swim. This is brand-new science that might show that *SPINOSAURUS* lived most of its life in the water!

BABY DINOSAURS LOOKED LIKE THEIR PARENTS

WRONG!

A lot of animals (like humans) look very similar to their parents when they are young, just smaller, but some animals only change to look like their parents when they grow up. By studying rare, special fossils, palaeontologists now know some young dinosaurs looked VERY different from their parents.

Scipionyx

Most young animals have big eyes – that's what makes some baby animals look cute to humans. *SCIPIONYX* is only known from one tiny fossil of a baby – and its large eyes meant it was definitely cute!

Ornithomimus

Some dinosaurs, like *ORNITHOMIMUS*, were covered in fluffy down as youngsters, and only grew large feathers when they were older.

Chasmosaurus

Fossils of baby dinosaurs with neck frills and head horns, like *CHASMOSAURUS* and *PROSAUROLOPHUS*, show that these parts of the body didn't grow bigger until they were older, and that they only had little nubs for horns when they were young.

Prosaurolophus

Mussaurus

Growing bigger sometimes means changing the way you move around. As the Triassic *MUSSAURUS* grew up, it went from walking on all four feet to using only two, while the Cretaceous *MAIASAURA* walked on two feet as a baby but on four when it had grown up.

Tyrannosaurus

Although *TYRANNOSAURUS* grew to be a huge predator with tiny arms, as a young dinosaur they would have been fluffier with longer arms. They also would have had miniature teeth in comparison to fully grown tyrannosaurs, so they would have hunted different, smaller prey.

A few palaeontologists today believe that some dinosaurs might not be different species, as first thought, but just younger or older versions of the same animals.

 DRACOREX, *STYGIMOLOCH* and *PACHYCEPHALOSAURUS* might all have been the same animal. As it grew, its horns grew smaller and smaller and its head dome grew thicker and thicker.

 NEDOCERATOPS and *TOROSAURUS* were huge horned dinosaurs and they might have been what *TRICERATOPS* grew into as it became very old.

 NANOTYRANNUS was a small, skinny theropod that was discovered in the 1980s. Although palaeontologists first thought it was a new species, scientists now think *NANOTYRANNUS* was actually a teenage *TYRANNOSAURUS*!

Only by discovering more fossils and taking a *CLOSER* look at what these bones from the past are really telling us, can we discover more about how dinosaurs grew up – and how different they looked from their parents!

DINOSAURS SNAPPED THEIR JAWS LIKE CROCODILES

Chewing might not sound like an amazing ability, but it's actually an animal superpower.

All animals with jaws can move them up and down against each other at least a little bit, and this lets them bite prey, grab plants between their teeth, or groom themselves.

The ancestors of mammals like giraffes, humans, mice and opossums first evolved in the Triassic period, and they brought an amazing new skill to the world.

These new mammals had special bones that let their jaws move in a different way – they could move their bottom jaws from side to side. Give it a try! From mice to mammoths, hyenas to hedgehogs – almost all mammals are able to chew.

Aquilarhinus

giraffe

Limusaurus

Dinosaurs, on the other hand, could only move their jaws up and down. Sure, some dinosaurs, like *AQUILARHINUS*, had amazing crazy-looking shovel-mouths for scooping through aquatic plants and some, like *LIMUSAURUS*, grew a beak as they became older, but no dinosaurs could mush up their food by moving their teeth left and right against each other, like you can today.

At least, that's what palaeontologists thought . . .

When palaeontologists look very closely at dinosaur teeth, they can see lines where the foods they ate scratched marks on their teeth. Different types of food leave different sorts of scratches and the directions of these scratches show how the teeth moved against each other!

Edmontosaurus

The cheeks were pushed out by the bottom teeth pushing the top teeth sideways!

What surprised palaeontologists so much was when they realised the marks on the teeth of *EDMONTOSAURUS* showed a side-to-side movement. Eating all that prehistoric vegetation was no problem for old Eddie!

Their skulls were packed with hundreds of teeth, and it looks like when the 'cow of the Cretaceous' took a bite downwards, the bottom teeth pushed the upper teeth out and sideways thanks to their jaws having hinges, pushing them out into its cheeks.

So, in a totally different way to mammals, dinosaurs evolved their own way to chew their food and break it down into more easily digested grub.

THEROPODS ONLY ATE MEAT

Theropods like *TYRANNOSAURUS*, *ALLOSAURUS* or *DAKOTARAPTOR* were fearsome predators – meat-eating hunters with sharp teeth that could slice through flesh.

But one group of theropods – the therizinosaurs – lived a very different sort of life during the Cretaceous period.

Therizinosaurs confused palaeontologists when they were first discovered because of their bizarre bodies, but now we have a much better idea of what sort of animals they were.

Neimongosaurus

NEIMONGOSAURUS' teeth were very different from those of meat-eating theropods. The teeth in its lower jaw had jagged edges like a saw, and would have been great for biting and eating plants.

Alxasaurus

ALXASAURUS was an early member of this group of dinosaurs. Like other therizinosauroids, it had wide hips which held up a big pot belly. This big belly held a large stomach that broke down their favourite vegetarian foods.

Therizinosaurus

Beipiaosaurus

BEIPIAOSAURUS was one of the smallest therizinosauroids. It probably ate plants as well and, like many other theropods, was covered in fluffy down.

THERIZINOSAURUS was one of the largest ever theropods. Its huge claws would have been useful for grasping leaves and, millions of years later, the giant ground sloths would evolve to live and eat in a very similar way.

Although people originally thought these were monstrous animals, slowly palaeontologists have pieced together an odd collection of animals – vegetarian, pot-bellied, long-armed, fluffy giants.

When animals eat a particular type of food, their diet can be recorded in the shape of their mouths, teeth and other parts of their body. A number of theropods 'specialised' to eat different sorts of food – not just other dinosaurs . . .

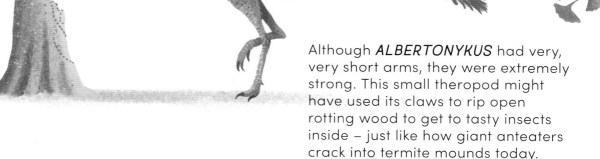

Albertonykus

Although **ALBERTONYKUS** had very, very short arms, they were extremely strong. This small theropod might have used its claws to rip open rotting wood to get to tasty insects inside – just like how giant anteaters crack into termite mounds today.

Masiakasaurus

Some dinosaurs had more mysterious mouths. What *MASIAKASAURUS* ate is, for now, a mystery as no animal has teeth that stick out quite like this today.

The humpbacked *DEINOCHEIRUS* was a mystery for 50 years when only its arms and blunt claws had been found. Eventually more of its skeleton was discovered and its wide mouth and the remains of its meals showed that it ate fish and plants – so it probably lived on riverbanks or beside lakes.

Deinocheirus

Majungasaurus

MAJUNGASAURUS lived on what is now the island of Madagascar and some of their fossilised bones have been discovered with bite marks in them from other *MAJUNGASAURUS*. Were they scavenging members of their species that had already died? Or did these animals live – at least sometimes – as cannibals?

So not all theropods ate meat, and some of them looked very strange! We need to keep digging to discover more about animals we still don't quite understand – like *MAJUNGASAURUS* and *MASIAKASAURUS*. It took palaeontologists a long time to find out what *DEINOCHEIRUS*'s arms were attached to, so sometimes patience pays off!

RAPTORS SLASHED THEIR PREY

WRONG!

**Let's start off on the right foot – or claw!
'Raptors' are modern-day birds.**

Velociraptor

Birds of prey, from snowy owls to harpy eagles and gyrfalcons, have been called 'raptors' by people since the early nineteenth century. It's only been since the late twentieth century that people have been calling dromaeosaurid dinosaurs 'raptors', using the end part of their long scientific names (like *VELOCIRAPTOR*).

One of the most famous parts of these dinosaurs is their terrifying toe.

Most people think it was only dromaeosaurids like *VELOCIRAPTOR* that stalked prey with their toe held upright, protecting a long, sickle-shaped blade-like claw. But a host of early paravians (the group of animals that includes birds and their dinosaur relatives) also featured this famous toe.

So animals like *XIXIASAURUS* and the long-legged *HESPERORNITHOIDES*, as well as dromaeosaurs like *BUITRERAPTOR* and the enormous *UTAHRAPTOR*, also had large, sickle-shaped claws.

But did they really use these weapons to slash and cut open their prey?

Xixiasaurus

Hesperornithoides

Buitreraptor

Utahraptor

DINO FACT!

All dinosaurs walked on their toes. In fact, it's actually quite weird that humans don't, and it's quite unusual for our ankles to touch the floor.

The best way to answer this is to look at modern-day dinosaurs as lots of modern raptors still have sickle-shaped claws on their feet – we call these talons.

None of these animals use their claws to slash or cut open their prey. Instead, they use their claws to hold on to their prey – usually pinning them to the floor and standing on top of them!

Some palaeontologists have even built models of dromaeosaur feet and experimented to see whether they were any good at slicing through things and, it turns out, they're not very good at all!

There were many other types of strange dinosaur feet:

harpy eagle

Balaur

BALAUR was one of the oddest of the sickle-claw-sporting dinosaurs . . . it had TWO sickle claws on each foot!

Vespersaurus

Animals that move swiftly often have very light limbs and evolve simpler feet through time. The very recently discovered *VESPERSAURUS* ran around its desert home on just one toe – like horses do today.

Centrosaurus

Some dinosaurs, like **CENTROSAURUS**, walked on claws that had actually evolved into hooves! The enormous sauropods still walked on their tiptoes, but the rest of each foot was supported by a large, fleshy, fatty pad – just like elephants today (yes, elephants walk on their toes)!

Although dinosaurs with sickle-shaped claws probably didn't slash their prey with them, they would have been useful tools that could have been used for many tasks. Remember, it's difficult to describe the behaviour of an animal just from one part of its body and it's important not to get too carried away with guesses when you only have a little information!

DINOSAURS COULD BE BROUGHT BACK TO LIFE

Pretty much everyone would like a pet *PROTOCERATOPS* wouldn't they? Or a ride to school on a *CAMARASAURUS*? But would it ever be possible to bring extinct non-bird dinosaurs back from the dead?

Protoceratops

Camarasaurus

One way some scientists think they can 'de-extinct' animals from the past is to put some of their DNA into the eggs of closely related animals alive today.

DNA is a chemical found in all living things that contains the instructions for how to build a particular animal, plant or other organism. By putting those instructions into the egg of another similar animal, maybe it would be possible to ride a *KAMUYSAURUS* to maths class . . .

Unfortunately, DNA only lasts for about one million years at the very most, and only in tiny amounts, so dinosaur DNA from at least 66 million years ago is highly unlikely ever to be found.

So we probably can't use dinosaur DNA, but is there another way we could try to 'make' a dinosaur?

Scientists have already discovered that by turning on and off certain bits of DNA at different times, chickens can grow a toothy snout rather than a horny beak! A few scientists think that by cleverly changing how birds grow from chicks, when they are very young, it would be possible to make them grow in the same way their dinosaur ancestors did.

DNA is a long, spiral string called a double helix.

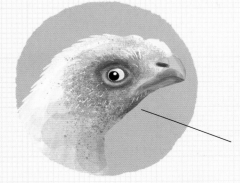

But would changing its face be a nice thing to do to a chicken? Maybe it would find eating difficult with a stubby face, and what if it made breathing hard? Questions like this – about 'ethics' and animal welfare – are really important to think about in science before any experiments are done.

What a dino-engineered chicken could look like.

Teeny TINY traces of other ancient chemicals can still be found in extremely rare cases. In fact, just a few years ago a team of scientists discovered fossilised dinosaur blood! They had placed some dinosaur bone under an amazingly high-powered microscope for a totally different reason and then spotted it by accident!

Some palaeontologists think they have found other chemicals in dinosaur bones too, like small amounts of collagen (which helps build muscles and other parts of the body) in the sauropod *LUFENGOSAURUS*, which lived 195 million years ago! That's older than anyone thought microscopic soft things could possibly last for.

Lufengosaurus

So, although scientists can't bring back a whole dinosaur, we can find out more secrets about them by discovering ancient chemicals trapped in fossils . . . and maybe build a chicken that at least looks like a dinosaur!

WE'VE ALWAYS KNOWN WHAT DINOSAURS LOOKED LIKE

WRONG!

Palaeontologists have been digging up fossils for hundreds of years but that doesn't mean they have always known how those bones fitted together. It's only by discovering more and more remains that scientists can be sure that their reconstructions are correct!

When the first sauropods were discovered, some biologists tried to imagine how these huge animals could have walked – how did their legs move under such great weight? But the biologists spent too long looking at lizards alive today. Living reptiles walk in a 'sprawling' style, which means their legs stick out to the sides as they walk, and that's how Gustav Tornier, a German zoologist, drew them in his illustrations in 1910.

As more and more dinosaurs were discovered, palaeontologists started to realise that dinosaurs walked with their legs straight, underneath them – and that sauropods didn't really drag their bellies on the floor!

IGUANODON was first imagined to be a rhinoceros-like animal, with a horn on the end of its nose (which was later discovered to be a thumb spike). Only after more remains were uncovered were the animals more correctly reconstructed – although the 'kangaroo' pose that many museums then displayed the animals' bones in was still wrong!

Some very inventive people once even believed *STEGOSAURUS* used its plates as wings that let it glide through the air! But this idea never really got off the ground . . .

Some palaeontologists and palaeo-artists during the last century thought that the super-tall sauropods, such as *BRACHIOSAURUS*, wouldn't have been able to support their huge weight, so they must have lived in the water in order to float. Modern palaeontologists are sure this is not correct, though, and that *BRACHIOSAURUS* and its relatives did indeed roam the land.

It's easy to smirk at palaeontologists and their ideas from the distant past, but palaeontologists today can still make mistakes. At the end of the twentieth century, scientists were so excited to find dinosaurs with feathers, a dinosaur nicknamed '*ARCHAEORAPTOR*' was announced to the world – but it was later discovered to be a fake. It was actually three dinosaurs and ancient birds stitched together!

Today, if you pick up some older books about dinosaurs, you still might see some of these mistakes in the pictures. And who knows? One day, you might even discover some mistakes in this book, as new discoveries about what dinosaurs looked like are being made all the time . . .

WE'VE FOUND ALL THE DINOSAURS

 WRONG!

We've discovered them all? Not even close! Right now, people are discovering new types of dinosaurs faster than ever before. There's never been a more exciting time to be a palaeontologist!

People have been stumbling upon dinosaur bones for thousands of years and the first myths about dragons in China were probably fuelled by their discovery.

The first dinosaurs to be found and described in Europe – *MEGALOSAURUS* and *IGUANODON* – were discovered in the UK.

AROUND 2000 YEARS AGO

AROUND 1824

The 'Bone Wars' were waged between Edward Drinker Cope and Othniel Charles Marsh – two palaeontologists who competed to be best in the world. *TRICERATOPS*, *DIPLODOCUS*, *STEGOSAURUS* and *COELOPHYSIS* were all discovered by their teams of fossil hunters.

The fossil bird *ARCHAEOPTERYX* was discovered in Germany.

The word 'Dinosauria' was invented by Sir Richard Owen, a biologist who would one day help build the Natural History Museum in London.

1877 to 1892

1861

1841

The sensational first fossils of *SPINOSAURUS* were discovered in Africa but later destroyed in the Second World War.

VELOCIRAPTOR was discovered in the Gobi Desert and, the following year, the first dinosaur eggs.

The giant predator *TARBOSAURUS* was discovered in Mongolia.

1915

1924

1955

TYRANNOSAURUS's cousin *THANATOTHERISTES* – meaning 'reaper of death' – was named, 10 years after being discovered in Alberta, Canada.

PATAGOTITAN, the largest dinosaur ever found, was discovered in Argentina.

The first non-bird dinosaur with feathers was discovered – *SINOSAUROPTERYX*.

TODAY **2020**

2008

1996

52

The number of dinosaurs we know about just keeps growing!

Yehuecauhceratops

More than 50 new types of frill-crested ceratopsians have been discovered since 2000!

Brasilotitan

And more than 40 new types of the truly gigantic long-legged dinosaurs known as titanosaurs – the biggest dinosaurs ever to live – have been found in the last 10 years, and all of them in South America.

Laiyangosaurus

More than 100 new types of dinosaurs have been discovered in China since the early 1990s!

In fact, all together, half of all the different types of dinosaurs we know about were only discovered in the last 10 years . . .

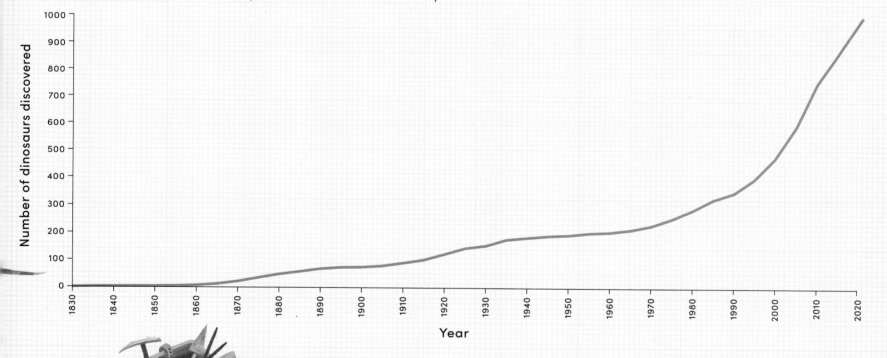

One of the reasons why more dinosaurs are being discovered today is that palaeontologists have better tools, but they are also digging in more places. They have only just started digging beneath the surface of the Earth in countries like Brazil where dinosaurs like *BAGUALOSAURUS* (2018) have been found.

Even though we have discovered over 1000 different types of dinosaurs over the last 200 years, there are hundreds of thousands of dinosaur fossils still waiting to be discovered under the earth, and the strangest-looking, most interesting dinosaurs are still locked in the ground. Who knows what secrets they will reveal . . . ?

THERE'S NO SUCH THING AS A *BRONTOSAURUS*

If you asked your parents whether *BRONTOSAURUS* was a real dinosaur, some really smart ones might say, "No! *BRONTOSAURUS* was really *APATOSAURUS*" and then they might show you lots of books that say that . . . and then they'll look all smug and pleased with themselves . . .

But here's the truth . . . *BRONTOSAURUS* was described in 1879, at the height of the Bone Wars and for a while everyone was happy with this newly described 'Thunder Lizard'.

But, a palaeontologist in the early 1900s took a look at the '*BRONTOSAURUS*' skeleton and said that it was actually just another skeleton of a dinosaur that had already been named two years before – the similar looking *APATOSAURUS*. *BRONTOSAURUS* is a great name (and it's easier to say!), so people kept using it even though scientists had said it wasn't real.

But THEN, in 2016, a team of scientists carefully looked at all the *DIPLODOCUS*-like dinosaurs and discovered that lots of details had been missed – the back bones of *BRONTOSAURUS* were different from *APATOSAURUS*, it was smaller, and its skull didn't look the same at all . . . *BRONTOSAURUS* had been real the whole time!

125 years after it was first found, *BRONTOSAURUS* was brought back!

When palaeontologists describe new types of dinosaurs only to find out later that they were the same as dinosaurs that had already been discovered, the new names they invented become extinct.

During the Bone Wars, many other dinosaurs were named that weren't really new types. '*CREOSAURUS*', described in 1878, was really just an *ALLOSAURUS*.

This happened in the twentieth century too. '*BRONTORAPTOR*' was described in 1996 but was later found to be a fossil of the Late-Jurassic theropod *TORVOSAURUS*.

Sometimes palaeontologists only find one bone and name a whole new dinosaur. '*ULTRASAUROS*' was named after a huge back bone that was later worked out to have actually belonged to the gigantic *SUPERSAURUS*. Oops!

1.33 m

PALAEONTOLOGISTS SPEND THEIR DAYS DIGGING

Dinosaur experts don't really spend all their time scrabbling around on their hands and knees looking for fossilised teeth, bones and claws. Being a palaeontologist actually means doing all kinds of different jobs.

VISIT MUSEUMS AND STUDY FOSSILS

Many, many dinosaurs have already been found, but we don't know everything about them. So, palaeontologists spend a lot of their time investigating fossils kept in museums. Taking pictures of them and drawing their bones very carefully can help them discover new facts about the animals – even though they might have been kept in a drawer or a cupboard for years!

WATCH ANIMALS ALIVE TODAY

By studying animals that are alive today, like birds and reptiles, scientists can get a much better idea of how dinosaurs might have behaved around each other.

X-RAY FOSSILS

Sometimes it is very difficult to take all the extra rock off a fossil, so scientists use powerful X-rays to look inside them. This means palaeontologists can look inside a rock and spot the dinosaur's remains – just like a doctor can use X-rays to see bones inside you at a hospital!

USE COMPUTER MODELS AND 3D PRINTING

Palaeontologists can use these X-rays to make models of dinosaurs using special computer programmes. Then they can 3D print models and play with them to discover how dinosaurs might have moved all of their bones around when they were alive!

SPEND LOTS OF TIME IN PREPARATION LABS

When palaeontologists DO spend time digging up fossils, the bones they find are usually attached to a lot of rock. This all needs to be cleaned off carefully with drills, saws and chemicals.

WATCH HOW THINGS ROT

It's important to understand what happened to dinosaurs after they died, but before they became fossils. Some palaeontologists study how animals rot . . . which can be very smelly work.

TEACH

Lots of palaeontologists teach people about the history of life on Earth or how animals' bodies work, and give talks at museums and schools. They are usually really keen to talk to anyone about their favourite dinosaur!

DO COMPLICATED MATHS

Some palaeontologists use maths to recreate ancient worlds inside their computers to discover what the climate was like, and what it must have been like to walk in prehistoric forests or deserts.

WRITE

Palaeontologists also spend a lot of their time writing. They write all of their discoveries into long articles that get published in special magazines for scientists, called journals.

FINALLY . . .

Sometimes it's tricky to understand things on your own, so it's a great idea to chat to your friends about it. Because of this, palaeontologists also spend their days reading what other scientists have written and talking to other palaeontologists so that they can answer the hardest questions together.

DINOSAURS ARE JUST FOR BOYS

It doesn't matter who you are or where you're from . . . dinosaurs are for everyone!
Some people might think only boys like dinosaurs, but in fact, some of the greatest
dinosaur palaeontologists working today are women!

SUSIE MAIDMENT

Susie is a British palaeontologist who researches stegosaurs and their relatives at the Natural History Museum, London. Her favourite place to do fieldwork is Utah in the USA for the beautiful natural environment. (And also for amazing breakfast burritos!)

SANAA EL-SAYED EL-BASSIOUNI

Sanaa is an Egyptian vertebrate palaeontologist who helped discover *MANSOURASAURUS*, a sauropod from the Cretaceous of Africa. (Which was the first time in the history of Egypt there was an Egyptian team unearthing an Egyptian dinosaur!)

VERÓNICA DÍEZ DÍAZ

Verónica is a Spanish palaeontologist who uses computer simulations to work out how the enormous sauropod dinosaurs moved. She also plays the trombone . . . and the banjo!

CECILIA APALDETTI

Cecilia is an Argentinian palaeontologist who studies some of the earliest giant dinosaurs from the Triassic period.

YARA HARIDY

Yara is an Egyptian palaeontologist who grew up in Canada. She studies how bones and teeth evolved and how dinosaurs healed after being injured. She loves to hike and go birdwatching.

JINGMAI O'CONNOR

Jingmai is an American-born palaeontologist who works in China on some of the earliest birds and their dinosaur relatives. She has two dogs and loves to sing Irish folk songs.

PIA VIGLIETTI

Pia is a South African palaeontologist who works on fossil sites in the Karoo Basin, South Africa, and many other countries in Africa, where she tries to better understand the world at the end of the Triassic period.

SARAH KEENAN

Sarah is an American palaeontologist and geochemist who studies how bones turn into fossils. She once found a *TRICERATOPS* which she, obviously, nicknamed TriSarahTops.

JASMINA WIEMANN

Jasmina is a German palaeontologist who studies the soft tissues in fossils to learn more about how dinosaurs behaved, lived and evolved. Her most exciting discovery was extracting cells from *ALLOSAURUS* bones!

LINDSAY ZANNO

Lindsay is an American palaeontologist who spends lots of her time in the field in the western US excavating dinosaurs out of very hard rock – usually with jackhammers and saws!

FEMKE HOLWERDA

Femke is a palaeontologist from the Netherlands who is an expert on Jurassic sauropods. She has studied the enormous *PATAGOSAURUS* from Argentina, and has to travel a lot to Patagonia.

ANUSUYA CHINSAMY-TURAN

Anusuya is a South African palaeontologist who has studied and written about dinosaurs in Africa and the complicated biology of how their bones grew.

DUANGSUDA CHOKCHALOEMWONG

Duangsuda is a Thai palaeontologist who helped discover *SIAMRAPTOR* in 2019, the first carcharodontosaur to be found in South East Asia. She believes anything is possible if you're brave enough!

KIERSTEN FORMOSO

Kiersten is an American palaeontologist who studies the large marine reptiles that dinosaurs lived with. She plays the trombone and piano, and roots for her university's American football team.

EMILY RAYFIELD

Emily is a British palaeontologist who uses engineering computer programmes to work out how dinosaurs lived, ate and moved.

GABI SOBRAL

Gabi is a Brazilian palaeontologist who studies the insides of the skulls of lots of animals, including dinosaurs like *DYSALOTOSAURUS*. She loves to hike and go rock climbing.

EMMA DUNNE

Emma is an Irish palaeontologist who uses computers to investigate how ancient climate might have affected where dinosaurs lived and how they evolved.

EUGENIA GOLD

Eugenia was born in Argentina and is a palaeontologist who studies brain evolution in birds and dinosaurs and co-wrote the book *She Found Fossils*, all about amazing women in palaeontology.

BOLORTSETSEG MINJIN

Bolortsetseg is a Mongolian palaeontologist who, as well as discovering new fossils, works to bring dinosaurs that were illegally taken from Mongolia back to her home country.

ELENA CUESTA

Elena is a palaeontologist from the Canary Islands who studies theropods discovered in Spain and Asia. In her spare time, she studies Japanese and loves to play video games.

NOW WE KNOW IT ALL

By the time you have finished reading this book, a lucky palaeontologist may well have discovered a brand-new type of dinosaur. Or they may have stumbled across a new specimen of a type of dinosaur we already know about.

With every new discovery – whether it's a whole skeleton or just a fragment of a single bone – comes new knowledge. Each new fossil, no matter how small or incomplete, can tell us a tiny bit more about whatever sort of animal it was.

These new, small pieces of information slowly help palaeontologists see a more complete picture of what dinosaurs were really like – how they looked after their young, how they moved, what colours they were. But there is still so much we have yet to learn! Palaeontologists continue to search for fossils in new parts of the world, use new technology to study old specimens, and stalk the halls of museums to redescribe skeletons that have been stored away for years.

And with each new discovery we get closer to knowing the **TRUTH** about what dinosaurs were really like. But remember, facts can be proven wrong! Not so long ago, many people thought *TYRANNOSAURUS* could outrun you, that most dinosaurs were cold-blooded, and that there was no way some dinosaurs were covered in fluff.

So, one day, maybe, we might find out that some of the things we think about dinosaurs **TODAY** – even some of the facts in **THIS** book - might be **WRONG** too!

GLOSSARY

ALVAREZSAURIDS A group of small, two-legged dinosaurs with tiny but powerful arms that lived during the Late Cretaceous.

ANCESTOR A species of animal or plant that another, later animal or plant is related to.

ARCHOSAUR A group of animals related to each other that includes birds, crocodiles, alligators and caiman today, and other extinct animals like non-bird dinosaurs and rauisuchians.

BIOLOGIST A scientist that studies living things, such as plants, animals and fungi.

BONE WARS A period of time at the end of the nineteenth century during which many well-known dinosaurs were discovered in North America by teams of palaeontologists.

CAMOUFLAGE The ability of some animals to escape being noticed by being coloured a similar way to their backgrounds.

CANNIBAL An animal that eats other animals of the same species.

CARNIVORE An animal that eats other animals.

CERATOPSIANS Herbivorous dinosaurs with frilled skulls, bony beaks and sometimes horns.

DNA Deoxyribonucleic acid: a chemical code found in most cells of animals, plants, fungi and other living things that contains instructions on how to control and build a body out of chemicals called proteins.

DROMAEOSAURIDS A family of fast-running, two-legged dinosaurs with sickle-shaped claws on their second toes.

EVIDENCE Pieces of information which show whether an idea is true.

EVOLVE When the average behaviour or body of a species changes through time between generations.

EXCAVATE To take out of the ground.

EXTINCTION When the last animal or plant of a species dies.

FOSSIL The mineral remains of an animal that died millions of years ago. Fossils may be of the animal itself, its dung, its eggs, or an impression or trace it left.

GEOLOGICAL Something related to rocks or the study of the Earth.

HADROSAUR Large, herbivorous, 'duck-billed' dinosaurs that lived during the Cretaceous Period.

HERBIVORE An animal that eats plants.

HYPOTHESIS An answer to a problem which is shown to be either true or false following the collection of evidence.

MAMMALS A group of animals with backbones that have fur, produce milk and generate their own heat.

MICROSCOPE A piece of scientific equipment which magnifies small things to make them appear bigger and easier to see.

OLFACTORY BULB Part of the brain that detects smells by receiving signals from the mouth and nose.

ORGANISM A single living thing, such as a single *Triceratops*, a single silver birch tree, or a single bacterium.

ORNITHOPODS A group of usually large, beaked, herbivorous dinosaurs that became very widespread in the Cretaceous Period.

ORNITHISCHIAN 'Bird-hipped'. One of the two main types of dinosaurs defined by palaeontologists in the nineteenth century.

PALAEONTOLOGIST A scientist who studies fossilised animals from the past and the world in which they lived.

PREDATOR An animal that hunts and eats other animals.

PREY Animals hunted and eaten by predators.

REPTILES A group of animals with backbones that includes lizards, snakes and tuatara, turtles, and crocodiles, alligators and caiman. Birds are also now understood to be reptiles.

SAURISCHIAN 'Lizard-hipped'. The other of the two main types of dinosaurs defined by palaeontologists in the nineteenth century.

SAUROPODS A group of dinosaurs that had long necks, long tails and often grew to very large sizes.

SECOND WORLD WAR A war that lasted from 1939 to 1945 that involved many countries from all over the world, and resulted in the deaths of millions of people.

SPECIMEN An individual or part of an individual animal, plant, or fossilised remains of one.

THERIZINOSAURS A group of two-legged, mainly herbivorous theropod dinosaurs.

THEROPODS A large group of hollow-boned, two-legged dinosaurs including Tyrannosaurus rex and all modern birds.

VEGETATION A collection of plants found in an environment.

ZOOLOGIST A scientist that studies animals alive today.

INDEX

INDEX